Art in New England (with Sid and Manny)

by

David Macpherson

An Introduction

Retiring after forty years at the same job. That seems like such a great reward. No more work. You have nothing you need to do with yourself. You can do anything. You can put off the boring shit until tomorrow. You have a lot of tomorrows to push things onto.

Retiring after forty years at the same job. That can be a nightmare.

Take our family friend, Sid. After forty two years working the road crew, he now was single and at liberty. He was miserable. We didn't know that. He never told us how bored and useless he felt. He didn't feel that that was anyones business to know. Besides, retirement is supposed to be terrific.

He didn't golf. He didn't have too many friends. He didn't want to be stuck watching game shows or Fox News all day. The Bruins were always good to watch, but that's only eighty games a year, and most of them are at night.

He told me later, there was a lot of day drinking. There were some days he got so drunk, he didn't make it to watch the Bruins. This was all burdens he didn't feel he should share.

Then, one day, without realizing why, he went to the Worcester Art Museum. It was one of their free days. He went. He spent all day. That night he called me up. "Dave, you like this art shit, right?"

"Art shit? I like art, Sid. Yeah. I don't know if I would call it art shit, though."

"Good. I've decided that I want to do art for a hobby. And I need your help."

"If I can help, I will. But I have to tell you, I like looking at art. I don't make it. So I don't know if what I can offer will help you out."

"Do you want me to explain art to you?" I asked.

He got upset with that and went a little nutty. "I just need a driver who is willing to take me once a week to see some things. Go to museums. Go to galleries, but I figure more museums than galleries.

Galleries are about selling shit, and I'm about looking at the stuff. Besides, the good stuff is in museums and I ain't interested in second rate product."

With such a glowing response, how could I say no? I took him to a few places, but he didn't seem happy. He wanted to talk to me and bitch about the art right while we were looking. I didn't want to talk while at the museums and Sid accused me of being a monk sworn to silence. "I thought you didn't want me to explain the art to you," I said.

"And I don't, but what's wrong with a little conversation? I don't want to wait for the car. I want to talk. Talking is a part of the experience, right?"

"For you maybe."

Sid came up with the solution. His friend, from the darts league, was also retired and wasn't too engaged. "Manny's going to come with us. Manny can talk. Hell, he was kicked off the dart team because he woudln't shut the fuck up while we was playing. He says he's up for this art thing. Manny likes the idea that there are bars and restaurants near the museums. He likes the idea of not just exploring art but new places to eat and drink. He's for all the arts he tells me."

I said it was fine and that I would give the two of them a year of my time and my gas for this project. "A year is probably too long, but that's good that you are willing, Dave," Sid told me.

The boys always rode in the back. They never called me a chaufeur, but I kind of felt like one. But it was nice to have a reason to go and see art I wouldn't see otherwise.

Now I must explain what I mean by calling this Art in New England. It doesn't mean all of New England. It mostly means Central Massachusetts and the Southern parts of Vermont and New Hampshire. There is a reason. Do you think I want to be in a car with the two of these guys all the way up to Bangor, Maine? Do you think they want to be in a car with me for that long, for the that matter?

Boston museums were out due to principle. Sid put his foot down about Boston by saying, "Do I really want to go to fucking Boston and make them think they are just so much more cultured than the rest of us, fuck no. They can have their MFA and their ICA and all the other three lettered bullshit places."

This is why a lot of the places we went to were in Worcester; they both live in Worcester, so why wouldn't they check out art there. We went to Brattleboro and the nearby towns too because Manny's daughter lives there and he always had us visit her after our trips to the museums and galleries were done.

What I have shared in this book is not all of the places we went to. Only some of them. Sometimes they had nothing to say. Sometimes it was the same things they said the museum before. I didn't have a recording device going, so this is as close as my memory can allow.

And if you ever find yourself in a gallery with two old guys in work boots and Bruins caps, don't you try to butt in with what they're saying or asking them to quiet down. There is no stopping them.

Brattleboro Museum, Brattleboro Vermont - The Scarf: Joan O'Beirne
January 20, 2018.

While the main space of the museum is taken with a bird of prey presentation with real birds of prey and seats full of wonder filled children, Manny and Sid give up the art in that room as a lost cause and check out the art that is not obstructed with families. They enter a gallery with one piece of work in it. There is a riser with steps that goes up six or seven feet. On the top is a chair. On the chair is an orange scarf that goes all the way down the steps to the floor and even further to the center of the gallery. At the top of the scarf, one of the knitting needles is still embedded into it.

Sid: Okay. A long scarf going off the chair onto the floor. Orange scarf. I sometimes don't get why art is art sometimes.

Manny: That's because it's not a scarf, it's a long extension power cord.

Sid: No, wait, it's what do you call it, yarn, and wait, holy shit. You're right, it's an extension cord. It's a cord from an extension cord.

Manny: That's what I said. Am I just talking to my own damn self?

Sid: That's crazy. I thought it was a scarf.

Manny: It is a scarf.

Sid: No it ain't. It's an extension cord. A hell of a lot of extension cord, but just a fucking cord. (He looks around for any spare kids running around before he says that last thing, Sid isn't a complete neanderthal)

Manny: Don't mean it ain't a scarf.

Sid: Sure it do. Scarves are yarn, like I said before. Yarn can do a lot, I guess, but it don't carry an electrical charge.

Manny: So what? Does a scarf have to be yarn?

Sid: Yeah.

Manny: Why? Really. Why? I mean we both came in and we saw the damn thing and what we think? We think, hey long scarf. So we saw it and said scarf. So, it's a scarf.

Sid: Bullshit. It's an electrical cord playing dress-up.

Manny: Okay. Scarves are yarn, but what about the ones made from fleece.

Sid: What about them?

Manny: Fleece is polyester. Oil product.

Sid: No shit? Fleece is polyester?

Manny: All day.

Sid: So what? It's made from oil, if you say so.

Manny: We call those scarves. First time they made one, they probably were crazed saying it wasn't a scarf, but people got over it. They got used to it. So what's to say that people won't get used to power cord scarves?

Sid: Because it's a goddam power cord. Scarves keep the neck warm. Look at that thing. It might look nice and orange, but it ain't going to do the job of a scarf. It's a power cord.

Manny: I don't know, maybe in the future. Maybe they will need it to get electricity. Maybe scarves will be different.

Sid: Then it will be something else and we won't call it a scarf.

Manny: (He looks over at the live bird of prey show in the larger gallery) You think one of those owls is going to escape and come over here?

Sid: I hope not. They better not.

Manny: But who's to say?

They look at each other and leave the museum without looking at any of the other galleries. They must not like raptors or extension cords. Either way, they eat at the burger joint up the hill.

Norman Rockwell Museum - Stockbridge, Massachusetts. Gloria Stoll Karn - Pulp Romance

February 16, 2018.

Another snowy day, but we find a way to make it to the museum. The exhibit features a female artist who painted covers for the pulp magazines of the 1940s. She painted a lot of woman bound in jeopardy from a hunchbacked fiend type covers for Dime Detective Magazine, but those original paintings are not the focus of the exhibit. She did many romance pulp covers; To be more precise she did covers for cowboy romance magazines. It was a thing, I guess. The paintings show rosy cheeked beauties being almost kissed by a guy in a cowboy suit. The canvases are large and bright and engaging. They seem to never be completely kissing in the paintings. All we see are almost lip contact, as if the cover was saying that for contact you had to slap your dime down, buy the magazine and read the damned story. One of the pictures shows a beautifully clean young woman with well washed hair and perfect skin smile as the guy with the bandana and the plaid flannel shirt almost kissed her. The boys planted in front of this one.

Sid: This ain't art.

Manny: What the hell are you talking about?

Sid: I'm talking that this ain't art.

Manny: That's what I thought you said. Still don't make a fuck of sense. I mean we are in an art museum. Looking at canvases nailed up to the wall. How the fuck is that not art? No really, Sid, how the fuck is that not art?

Sid: Because it's a painting for a cover to a magazine. That's not an art thing. That's just a magazine thing to sell copies. That's not art.

Manny: How come that ain't art?

Sid: Because it's a commercial thing. It is trying to sell something, a cowboy love story, that, let's be fair, no one really needs.

Manny: No one needs Mission Impossible movies, but I like to buy my tickets for them.

Sid: And would you call the movie poster for Mission Impossible art?

Manny: Yeah. If it got my eye and made me want to see another goddam Tom Cruise movie, then not only is it art, it is damn persuasive art at that.

Sid: These are commercials. These are all come ons.

Manny: And that's art. The cowboys are handsome. The girls are pretty in a soap commercial kind of way. They're doing cute things. That girl is selling Hershey Kisses and he's trying to rustle up a kiss himself. If I was the kind of guy that liked stories where cowboys fell in love with farmer's daughters selling candy from a bowl, then dammit all, I would buy that magazine. That's some powerful art that can make me do that.

Sid: Fuck that. It's still pictures trying to sell things. That's not art. Art is stuff made for the sake of making the stuff. It ain't going to sell cereal or magazines or advertise a nightclub. Art is the thing made to look at it and it alone. It's not a thing of commerce.

Manny: Now I call bullshit on that. Not a thing of commerce? Did the artist sell the painting for nothing? Did they give it away? Fuck no. They sold it for crazy money at Christies or the other one of those auction places. And you go to the museum gift shop and you can buy magnets and postcards and umbrellas with the image of that art for art sake on it. And they ain't giving that shit away for free neither.

Sid: But the artist didn't plan for their work to be all about money. It just happened.

Manny: Bullshit again. Bullshit all over. How do you know the artist didn't plan to make coin from what they was doing? I mean, give me these paintings any day. They had a purpose. They were to sell magazines. The magazine publisher kept on using this artist, so I guess she was successful, she sold magazines. With her paintings. With her art. And it wasn't just her making money from her cover art, but the writers and the editors and the printers. Because she made these cute paintings. Fuck what you call it. Call it art. Call it illustration. Call it advertising. Call it Carl from the Mailroom. I like it and you can go to hell.

Sid: I didn't say I didn't like it. I just said I don't think it's art.

The boys continue to be pissed at each other for the rest of the time at the museum. But by the time we eat pizza at a place in Great Barrington, all is forgiven. They are calling the pizza art at this point.

Pearl L. Crawford Library, Dudley, Massachusetts. Memorial Exhibit of the Art of David Omar White.

March 24, 2018

I get a call from Manny around noon on a Saturday, to Pick up Sid and get down to Dudley Mass to the Library. There is something good to see, he says. "Art." I sigh and do what I was told. He meets us at the entrance. As he leeds us to a small alcove where the paintings are, he says he was meeting an old friend here and now that was done and he wants us to see this art show that's here. He introduces us to six paintings by a Boston area artist who died about nine years ago. There are five watercolors of delicate unworldly landscapes. There is also are circular paintings that seem like scary fantasy emblems for the shields of Ork armies.

Sid: There are six paintings.

Manny: Pretty good, huh?

Sid: There are six paintings.

Manny: Quantity is not as important as quality.

Sid: That's the kind of thing someone who was annoyed they only got five fries with their fish and chips would hear. That's not the way art should be.

Manny: Sure it is. Libraries are alright places to see local art and the thing is sometimes they don't have a lot of space. They got to make due.

Sid: I drove forty minutes for six paintings.

Manny: You didn't drive. You were a passenger. Dave drove.

Sid: I was driven forty minutes for six paintings.

Manny: Dude, check out the art. You got six paintings, you can really spend the time looking at them.

Sid: You only do that if the art is worth the look.

Manny: Well look then, see what's here. It's good.

Sid: Yeah, it's good. But I am done looking at them in a few minutes. And now what?

Manny: You want gallery after gallery of mediocre art, or do you want two half walls of the good shit?

Sid: I think I want gallery after gallery of mediocre art.

Manny: That's bullshit.

Sid: No, because the large museum might have fair to middling shit there, but you have to take the time to come to that conclusion. When you got more galleries to go into, there is that great hope that the good stuff is waiting for you. It's like when you hear the Power Ball is up to a hundred million and you buy yourself a ticket or three. You know you ain't going to win nothing, but the thoughts and dreams are pretty good to have. You are paying for the hope of a windfall, not the windfall. That's going into the next room at a big museum. It's holding a losing ticket before you know it's a loser.

Manny: Good art can be six things. Look at this one. It hurts your head. It makes you focus. Do you need more art?

Sid: If I have to travel all the way to Dudley, I want not only good paintings, I want a lot of them. I want a reason to come here.

Manny: Any art is worth it.

Sid: I still don't think that's it.

I hate to admit it, but Sid is right. Manny needs a ride. He met his friend, and he didn't want to get an Uber all the way back to Worcester. Sid swears so much, we are asked to leave. It might be the first time I have ever been kicked out of a library, with or without a lot of art on the walls.

April 14, The Gallery of New Hampshire Crafters, Concord New Hampshire

Fairy Tales Exhibit

This is a winning gallery for the boys just by walking in. The woman behind the counter doesn't say anything about their cups of Dunkin Donuts. Letting the boys have their coffee while around art, that makes this a stellar joint. Sid and Manny are in a corner where the heads of paper mache dragons are mounted to the wall. They hardly glance at them, for their focus is on a fabric collage a few feet down the wall. The placard for the collage states the artist used remnants from kimonos to make this abstract free-form piece of art. It is entitled, "I Wish Dragons Are Real."

Sid: I don't get it, why is that called I Wish Dragons Are Real? There are no dragons here.

Manny: The hell are you talking about? Look over there. Three dragons.

Sid: I'm not talking about that, they ain't called I wish Dragons are Real. They are just dragons with titles that don't piss me off. I'm talking about this one, with that title.

Manny: Why does it piss you off? It's just some slick cloth sewed together. Kind of nice.

Sid: Fine. It's nice. It don't offend the eye. That's fine. That's just hunky dory. What the hell does the title have to do with what I'm looking at?

Manny: Maybe she made it and it made her think of dragons.

Sid: So? Who cares? There are no dragons there. I see no dragons.

Manny: You have to use your imagination.

Sid: Why? Why do I have to use my imagination? Why do I have to do the work? Am I the artist?

Manny: No, you ain't, but you are part of the whole thing. Artist does her thing, and then we do the rest.

Sid: Sure, I get it. Part of it. I get it. And I'm looking at this fabric art thing and it ain't bad one bit, but then you get the title. The title isn't the art. The title is words that they throw up on top. It's like staining a chair. It don't change the chair, it just makes it look darker.

Manny: Stain also makes a chair look good enough for people to buy. The title helps a guy figure out what's going on.

Sid: No. The art is supposed to tell you what is going on. A title is like cheating. A title is like passing a note in class.

Manny: Bullshit there. The title is part of the art.

Sid: So why is there so many things we seen that is untitled? If titles are necessary, then that would never happen. But look around, there are some untitled things even here. Does that mean they ain't finished?

Manny: What you saying?

Sid: What I'm saying is that to me, and it's only to me, is that the artist here had a nice piece of art going and heard about a fairy tale show and she slapped on a fairy tale title to get in.

Manny: That's a shitty attitude, Sid. Can't you just say that to you, you're not seeing the connection?

Sid: I thought I just did.

The two move on. Manny puts some money in the donation box, like he does and they toddle off to a gyro and beer joint for lunch. All the gyros come with fries inside the sandwich. Both agree that this is a nice touch.

Brattleboro Art Museum, Brattleboro Vermont - Best of Springs Sprockets and Pulleys/Steve Gerberich

March 29, 2018

In the main room and a few other galleries, large kinetic sculptures are displayed. All are made from discard and junk. One of the sculptures has sign asking the museum goer to sit on an old stationary bike and peddle, causing a fan to blow which then caused birds and things to fly. There are a few where you press buttons and animals cavort and play. A pair of children skitter from sculpture to sculpture with enthusiasm, with two tired grandparents in tow. Manny and Sid stare at the exercise bike like it is going to jump up and bite them.

Sid: The guy wants us to sit on that?

Manny: What guy?

Sid: The artist. The guy. He wants us to sit on that thing?

Manny: To make it move, yeah.

Sid: My ass won't fit on that thing.

Manny: Maybe this is art for skinny people.

Sid: All art is art for skinny people. Hey, where are the paintings?

Manny: Maybe in a different part of the place.

Sid: No, last time we was here, there was paintings. Photos that kind of stuff. Stuff to hang on the wall. It had pictures of animals. I wouldn't mind seeing those again.

Manny: That was the last show, the last exhibit. Those are gone.

Sid: Nothing here is the same art than the last time we was here and that was like just a few months ago.

Manny: I guess they only do exhibits. All the space is for art for just a little bit of time. No, what you call it, permanent collection.

Sid: That's the stuff they always have and the stuff they always have up?

Manny: Yeah. Permanent. Haven't we done this same talk before?

Sid: We've done every talk before. And I'm sure the last time I said the same thing. I don't trust museums that change everything every couple of months.

Manny: You don't trust them?

Sid: No, I don't trust them. They can't keep anything from one time to another, then they must not know or care for what's good.

Manny: Some museums are about the exhibit. They want people to see as much new stuff as possible. I mean this is a small joint. What was it, an old train station, right?

Sid: Looks like.

Manny: Can't have a permanent collection taking up valuable real estate when you are small.

Sid: No. It's the coward's way. They don't trust the art they got.

Manny: I don't know what art they got, but I still think that's bullshit. Big and loud.

Sid: If they had masterworks in the store room, why they ain't showing them?

Manny: They probably don't have masterworks. Most of these places don't have masterworks. They have nice things that can be shown. But this museum wants to show as much of what's going on as they can. You want them to come every few months and get the same thing everytime? People won't come if they see the same shit every time. Gotta give the people variety. Or you won't get people.

Sid: If it was good shit. Why wouldn't they want to dedicate a space for it? If there was something good. I mean really good. Like killer, stuck in your head you want to see it again, good. Then people come all the time just to see it. The Mona Lisa. That is something to keep on the wall for good and ever.

Manny: Vermont don't have the Mona Lisa. America don't have the Mona Lisa. We have walls that can get a lot of art up there. I want to see different things. I might like something once, or even twice. But if I come back a third time and that thing is still on the wall, I am not thinking that they are doing that for my benefit. I am thinking that they are too lazy to change the pictures.

Sid: I get you, but nothing but temporary exhibits? It's like driving through a city and you get nothing but billboards. The billboards change. Driving through Worcester, they have those murals now. The murals don't change, and when I see them, I like it. I like seeing them again. I even like seeing the awful ones because I can get pissed off all over again and say, you think this is art?

Manny: When was the last time you paid attention to a billboard?

Sid: It's the point I'm making. The point. The reality of it, just the point.

They go off to look at art they have not seen before and probably never see again. They then have a lot of beer down the hill at Whetstone Station.

APE Gallery. Northampton, Massacushesetts. Right to Left/What's Left to Write by Ernesto Montenegro and Dr Foad.

May 12th, 2018

We walk into one of our goto galleries in Northampton. It is right next to a good Mexican place, so it became a routine: see some art, good or bad, and then walk a few steps down the road for a fat, tasty burrito. The gallery is small enough for them to take it in quickly and move on. There are several large classical paintings being written on. The placard explains that Ernesto Montenegro painted these as a mural for an oppulent apartment in Boston. The apartment has been sold and he got the paintings back. He decided to speak about conversation and the problems we are having. He invited a professor he knew named Dr. Foad who was originally from Iran. The idea was to have him write on the old paintings. He was to write thoughts and ideas in Farsi. Dr. Foad is on a stepstool using a paint marker. He places farsi words around the empty spaces of the paintings. A few are done already and the rest are slowly being filled with words that look like art. The boys watch this for ten minutes. Dr Foad climbs down from his ladder for a break and walks over to Sid and speaks to him. This shocks Manny, whose mouth dangles open. Nobody speaps to Sid on their own volition. Sid and the professor speak for a moment and Dr. Foad moves back to the ladder. We leave soon after and head into Bueno y Suano. We are seated, waiting for our food when Manny finally speaks.

Manny: What he say?

Sid: What who said?

Manny: The guy on the ladder. The graffiti artist.

Sid: That wasn't no graffiti artist. That was a college professor.

Manny: A college professor who is putting graffiti on somebody else's art.

Sid: The artist didn't mind. Fuck, he asked the professor to mark that shit up. Didn't you hear the original artist while we was there? He was talking to some student reporter about what this whole thing means. Fuck. Art meaning something. A cool thing is happening in an art gallery, does it have to have some greater fucking meaning?

Manny: To the artists? Sure. Always. This shit ain't for pretty looking. This is for serious thinking.

Sid: Bullshit

Manny: It might be, but that's how they think it. Now answer the fucking question. What the professor say to you when he stepped down from the ladder.

Sid: He asked me if I had something I wanted to have on the paintings.

Manny: He wanted you to say something and then he was going to write it on the art?

Sid: Yeah, he wanted to see if I had something and he would put it in farsi and then on the paintings.

Manny: What you tell him?

Sid: You think I have something to say that will be part of art?

Manny: I don't?

Sid: You don't.

Manny: You think you don't have words worth being art? Well words translated into farsi, but still fucking art. You speak enough for three sons of bitches and none of it is worth being immortalized.

Sid: Well, to think of it, a lot of me is worth immortalizing. Sure. But I don't know what is worth being put up there like that. I don't know. What should I say? Would I say the wrong fucking thing? Would I say something and they get pissed and throw my ass out, and your ass too, because you're with me. Shit. Do I need the pressure? Can't I just fucking look at the art and everybody is satisfied?

Manny: Okay, I get it. I don't know if I would have liked being put on the spot. Did you call him out, tell him to leave you the fuck alone?

Sid: What the hell are you talking about? Of course I didn't. What the fuck do you think I am, a fucking monster? I told him I didn't know what to say, to add to the paintings. That I just wanted to watch the art and I thought it was an amazing thing to watch the words being written on the art.

Manny: Really? You think it was an amazing thing?

Sid: Sure. I do. It was kind of worth it. Watching some boring mythology art changing into something else with all those Farsi words put on it. I don't know if I like the final product as much as I liked watching it turning into something else. Yeah. It was pretty fucking alright.

Manny: But you didn't want to be part of the art.

Sid: Why does everyone want to be part of the art? Fuck that. I'm looking at it. Isn't that enough? Isn't that enough fucking participation for anyone?

Manny: Less artists and more audience?

Sid: Yeah, more of that.

When the boys finish their food, they aim themselves over to the Smith College Museum.

Smith College Art Museum - Northampton, Massachusetts. Modern Images of the Body from East Asia.

May 12th, 2018

The show is a group exhibit. It presents many paintings, sculptures and prints of different aspects of body identification, all from Asia. The boys are moving through it all pretty quickly. I don't think they are engaged in it. They aren't being rude. They have learned how to feign polite interest by this time in their excursions of museums and galleries. Their movement through the galleryies is a little faster than usual. Then they reach the table that holds the "Rubber Man" by Xinglei Pan. This stopps them cold. The placard describes that this is a mold of the artist's body, cast in rubber. It was then emptied of the mold, making it look deflated. It is as if all the air was let out of the person. Everything is loose and floppy. Except for the penis, that still has a little bit of shape. It sticks out and up.

Manny: Whoa.

Sid: Damn. Someone is having himself a happy thought.

Manny: I don't know, but you just can't stop staring at it.

Sid: Yeah. There is a lot of art going on, but all I'm looking at is the dick right there.

Manny: The penis.

Sid: Yeah, like I said. The dick.

Manny: No, not like I said. I said penis. I didn't say dick.

Sid: Same difference. Dick. Penis. They are all just part of the pecker category.

Manny: But we're in a museum.

Sid: I know. I walked in with you.

Manny: You don't say dick at a museum. You say penis.

Sid: Who the fuck says?

Manny: Well it's a museum. It's not a bar. It's not looking at dirty pictures in the art section of the library. This is the big time, museum. This ain't a place to say dick when you can say penis.

Sid: But maybe you should. I mean look at that thing. That thing pointing at something or other. Do we really think the artist wants us to call it a penis. I don't think so. I think he was thinking dick.

Manny: Well, it would be in Chinese whatever he was saying it in. Does Chinese have words for penis and dick?

Sid: Every language has words for penis and dick.

They walk through the rest of the museum exhibit quickly, like they need to be somewhere.

Ye Olde Watering Hole - The Beer Can Museum, Northampton, Massachusetts, May 5th, 2018

This is twenty minutes after leaving the Smith College Museum. They saw the sign for this bar driving in. They wanted to go to the Beer Can Museum. "A museum I can fucking get behind," one of them stated. We enter and it is a bar. Instead of neon signs saying Budweiser on the wall, there is row upon row of beer cans. It is overwhelming to see all that aluminum, but the boys took it in stride, like they see that kind of thing everyday. The bar is mostly empty and the bartender is talking about her vacation to the Caribbean with regulars. The boys order domestic and are satisfied.

Sid: This ain't a museum.

Manny: No shit. You can't get shots and a beer at a museum.

Sid: That's bullshit. They have functions at museums all the time. They got bartenders working the corners of those things. With watered down booze, but it's still a place where you can get a shot and a beer.

Manny: If it ain't that, then what makes this not a museum? Outside of it being a fucking bar?

Sid: It ain't a museum because this is just a collection of cans. It ain't a museum with items, they are just on the wall.

Manny: Wait, you can't be a museum if you're a collection. I seen those art magazines, and there are some museums that are called the collection. So bullshit on that. Museums can be one man's shit that he wants to show off, why the hell not?

Sid: A cabinet of curiosities.

Manny: A what now?

Sid: You're talking about a cabinet of curiosities.

Manny: I am?

Sid: You are.

Manny: Good, I'm glad you're fucking telling me what I'm saying. I wouldn't know what's coming out of my mouth if you didn't clarify it for me.

Sid: Glad to help.

Manny: What the fuck is a cabinet of curiosities?

Sid: That's the collections you was talking about. Back two hundred years ago, the rich doctor or what not collected things. Stuff they picked up in their travels of the fucking continent. Weird shit that they was sure wasn't tourist crap. They then displayed them in a room. Galleries, you know. That was called a cabinet of curiosity, though they wasn't just cabinets. They was private museums of weird shit. So yeah, collections could be museums. There's a weird museum in Philly that has fucked up medical things that started as a cabinet of curiosity.

Manny: How the hell do you know that?

Sid: Seeing art ain't the only thing to this hobby. I read about art too. I don't always understand what I'm reading, but hell, I don't always understand the art I'm looking at neither.

Manny: So what you're saying is that this place with all the beer cans is a cabinet of curiosities?

Sid: No, it's a fucking bar.

Manny: Here we go again.

Sid: What I mean is that this is a collection on a wall. A collection on a wall is nice, if you like the thing they are collecting. You got to like what is being collected. Beer cans, comic books, hummel figurines, pez dispensers. You think that shit is awesome and you see a huge bunch of them, then that is a hell of a collection. Ain't a museum.

Manny: Pez dispensers, sure, that shit will never be worth a museum. But can't you say the same thing for paintings, or pottery, or photographs? You can say that shit is just a collection. But that's the kind of shit in a museum. So I got to know, because at this point I don't. I got to know, what the fuck makes a museum?

Sid: A gift shop. You got a gift shop, you got a museum.

Manny: Fair enough. I like looking at all these beer cans.
Sid: Yeah. There's a lot.

The Sprinkler Factory - Worcester, Massachusetts. Art Opening of Two Shows. June 2, 2018

I was able to get them up and about on a Saturday night, which is not their usual mode. But I told them that we weren't far from a few good bars and they were up for it. The large, former factory space, is divided into two art exhibits. One is a group show of abstract paintings and the other side is a solo show of large abstract expressionism paintings. The way the shows work here is that the artists supply the food and the gallery staff sell the beer and wine. The boys sit in chairs near a hallway leading to artist studios. They have plates of cheese and fruit balanced on their knees, while holding their beer.

Sid: I don't know what to do.

Manny: Eat a little of the cheese on the plate and then drink the beer. I don't have to explain that to you, do I?

Sid: No, asshole. I'm thinking about what to do when we're finished eating this.

Manny: Well, we get up and look at the art some more. That's what everyone is doing. You eat the food, then you go look at the art some more. It's the implied contract.

Sid: That's the problem. We go up and look at the art, sure, but which side of the gallery. Which show?

Manny: The one we like better. The show in the front of the space. Right?

Sid: That's the problem. Don't you see the problem?

Manny: Does it look like I see the fucking problem?

Sid: Okay. Two shows. Two tables for food. The group show has a table of food. The solo show has a table of food. Which table did we get our plates from?

Manny: The solo show. That one.

Sid: Right, because that spread was better.

Manny: Meats and cheeses and the fruit looks fresh. Course that's the one we eat from. We ain't monsters or nothing.

Sid: So now do you see my problem.

Manny: Nope.

Sid: Thick. Look, which is the better show?

Manny: The group show.

Sid: Right, and we liked the solo show's food better. We took their food. And we liked the other show's art.

Manny: Oh. I see.

Sid: Right.

Manny: We ate the solo show food so we should spend more time there. But we like the group show's art, so we are going to look at that again.

Sid: Should we have sucked it up and ate the group show's food instead.

Manny: But their cheese wasn't that great looking.

Sid: So we got the solo show cheese and hardly spent time looking at it.

Manny: I like these paintings better.

Sid: Me too.

Manny: I guess the question is, is this part of the contract? If I eat your food, do I have to look at your art?

Sid: Well we did that. We did look at the art.

Manny: But not as much as we looked at the other stuff.

Sid: Now the contract, does it specifically state that we have to spend a certain amount of time? Like for every piece of fruit you eat, you have to stay for two minutes looking at the painting.

Manny: I ate a lot of their fruit. Does that mean I have to look at the art I don't like for twenty minutes?

Sid: I don't think so. I think the contract is not that specific. I think the contract is look at the art, even for a little and you can have food.

Don't be a dick on eating all the food, but the food is yours within reason.

Manny: Yeah. I think so. I think that's what the contract says. It's kind of a shitty contract for the artist, but hell, I didn't write it, I'm just living by it.

Sid: Yeah, that's it. So we finish our food and look at the art we like. And no one will be pissed at us.

Manny: Right, the contract says so.

The Clark Institute of Art, Williamstown, Massachusetts. - The Art of Iron

June 22, 2018.

The boys go to the museum early, before the summer crowds infest the galleries and make it a general annoyance to be here. The gallery is a building of its own, like it is not good enough to be housed in the museum proper. But it's a show on iron work from France. Iron work. Man's art. The boys are as excited as they get to see it. They walk by store signs and gates and stop at a small iron work bat with a blue light glowing in its belly.

Manny: That can't be the original wiring. That's impossible.

Sid: Read the damned sign, why don't you? That was put in later. Read the fucking sign on the side of the thing. See, wired in the twentieth century.

Manny: I don't think it was wired right.

Sid: Fucking expert on wiring now.

Manny: What I'm saying is that this is an old thing and it shouldn't be updated to have wiring. That's all I'm saying.

Sid: That's not what you said though. You said it wasn't wired right. That's different.

Manny: I'm saying old things shouldn't be wired to make them new things. Not if they are going to be hung in a museum. If you are in a museum, you are the way you are supposed to be. Original. Museum things don't get upgrades. They don't get to be a cyborg art piece.

Sid: Cyborg?

Manny: Half machine, half art. You get placed in the museum, you have to be all art. You have to have it in your bones, there can't be any wires and shit about it. Got to be fucking pure, you know?

Sid: Not one bit. This bat was the sign for a cabaret. No words or nothing. Just some iron bat and you know that this was where the good shit was.

Manny: Where the booze and dancing girls are?

Sid: This is the old time French version of a neon sign of a shapely leg. You didn't need words to know that this was the strip club.

Manny: Wait, this iron bat. This is saying that it's a strip club?

Sid: Sure, that's what a cabaret was, so sure.

Manny: Bullshit. That's not a cabaret. That's just a club with dancing and singing.

Sid: Dancing and singing and naked girls. Sure. They probably dressed as bats to start with before the music started.

Manny: That's not a cabaret. Not one inch of it.

Sid: Sure it is.

Manny: You know I take it back. The bat ain't the one with the messed wiring. It's you.

The boys are silent for a bit and then go off to the other pieces. They grumble for a bit, but are in better spirits when they walk to town and order sandwiches at Pappa Charlie's. Manny has the Dr. Strangepork. Sid gets what he always gets, the Gene Shalit.

The Worcester Center for Craft Krikorian Gallery - Worcester, Massachusetts, Tess Barbato

July 21, 2018

A relaxed afternoon of beating the heat and moving as little as possible leads us to not leave Worcester. They pick the Gallery because it isn't too far from a Panera Bread. The show is of large canvases. They are photorealistic paintings of money: stacks of coins, crumpled hundred dollar bills, side views of rolls of bills. The large size and the realistic vision of the money create a strong contrast. The boys stand before one painting that presents a stack of different coins.The placard states its title as $3.05.

Sid: I hate pocket change.

Manny: That's not pocket change. That's just a stack of change. No pocket there at all.

Sid: But when you're done painting that stack of change, what do you do with it? You swipe it up and put it in a pocket. So it ain't pocket change at the moment, but it's pocket change to be. And I hate pocket change of any kind.

Manny: Nothing to hate; it's money. It gets you shit.

Sid: But does it? Does it really? I mean, who buys things with pocket change? No one. No one uses it. They all have it, in every goddamn pocket, but no one uses it.

Manny: I use it.

Sid: Well aren't you Mister Moneybags himself. Most people hate it. Because it's a pain to count out and it doesn't get you nothing. A coffee is three bucks.

Manny: Not at Cumby's, it's still a buck and I can use quarters to get a cup. You get your coffee at overpriced places. Don't blame pocket change because you pick the wrong place for a cup.

Sid: No one likes three dollars and five cents in change. You jingle when you walk. You're a goddamn Christmas Elf when you walk around with three dollars and five cents in your pocket.

Manny: It's a nice painting. I like these paintings.

Sid: I don't like the price she's selling it for.

Manny: How much she listing it at?

Sid: Two thousand dollars. Two grand for a painting of three dollars and five cents. That's a goddamn rip-off.

Manny: Not for someone who likes it. For someone who likes and has the money, it's fine.

Sid: Bullshit. If a painting shows three bucks and a little over, then that's what it should cost.

Manny: Now that's bullshit.

Sid: Don't blame me. Blame the artist. If she wanted to get paid, she should have painted a canvas full of quarters and silver dollars. Then she could charge the bank.

Manny: That's batshit stupid.

Sid: Who's going to spend two grand for a painting anyway?

Manny: Lot of people. Not me. But people with money who want to look at something they like.

Sid: You want to look at a painting of a stack of coins adding to three bucks and a nickel hanging in your house?

Manny: Not me on this one. There is also the fact that I don't have two grand.

Sid: What happens if this don't sell for two thousand by the time this show ends?

Manny: I don't know, the artist takes it home I guess.

Sid: Right, so it's just in her basement or the attic or somewhere. Sitting there. What's the painting worth?

Manny: You know, I watched you pay for a coffee with dimes and nickels the other day. You who hates pocket change.

Sid: Well, I got it out of my pocket now, didn't I?

They exit to the Panera, like they planned. And they pay with their debit cards.

Mitchell-Giddings Fine Art - Brattleboro, Vermont. Torin Porter.

August 3rd, 2018

It is a First Friday Art Walk where all the galleries and coffee shops with art on the walls open for an examination of the art. This is a light night for attendance, probably due to the torrential fits of rain. The boys are determined to go see some art. They say, the hell with weather. Rain never stopped a day of fishing and drinking, why would it stop an evening of art looking and drinking? That was the plan at any rate. Sid is soaked when they enter this basement gallery space. He thinks maybe this will be the only one they need to go to. For the half hour they are there, the boys and myself are the entire audience. "We should stay until others arrive," Manny says. "It be rude to the art if no one was looking." The featured show is the steel sculptures of Torin Porter. They are small and representational. Most of them have small steel people stretching out their steel appendages to interact with steel birds or trees. They are odd and enchanting. The boys stand before one in a corner. It is of a ladder that bends in its middle and circles in on itself. The placard announces that it is entitled, "Ladder Dreams."

Manny: That's what ladders dream. They dream of twisting into a spiral. I never knew that's what ladders dream of.

Sid: Asshole. Ladders don't dream.

Manny: That's what the sign says. It says that that is the dream of a ladder.

Sid: It's the title of a steel sculpture. It's not a headline in the Boston Globe. Art titles don't have to be true to life.

Manny: I kind of figured that. I ain't that big an idiot. But I was just digging the twisty ladder and the title. And I was thinking, that yeah, that's what ladders would dream.

Sid: Bullshit. A ladder is a straight shooter. A ladder dreams of people climbing it. A ladder dreams of a whole crew going up to do a roofing job. If there was a ladder nightmare, the dream would be one of the steps being rotten and a foot going through it. That's a ladder nightmare.

Manny: Nah. I like this being the dream. I like the dream of it curling.

Sid: But then it can't do ladder things. It wouldn't be a ladder if it did that.

Manny: That's what a dream does. It makes you other things. You can have wings. You can be a fish. You can vote the wrong way. That's what dreams are good for. You ain't nailed down to being you.

Sid: That's you talking. Not a ladder. A ladder is a meat and potato kind of dreamer. A ladder doesn't bend. In dreams or anywhere. People go up ladders. People go down them. Drunk people go sideways on ladders and then sue for workman's comp.

Manny: Your ladders do the job just fine I guess, but they got no art in them.

Sid: I know.

The rain stops for a time and the boys make a mad dash to get to the brewery that produces nothing but sour beer. They drink their samples and head out. "They're sour," one of them says. "They're supposed to be," the other say, but the next place they stopp they both have Heinekens and seem pleased enough.

Bennington Museum, Bennington, Vermont. Crash to Creativity: The New Deal in Vermont

August 4th, 2018

The first floor of the museum is full of Grandma Moses art. The boys cluck respectfully at what they se but arere happy to hear that there is art on the second floor. One of the shows is art produced in Vermont as part of the New Deal WPA program where the government paid for artists to work. They stop by a group of color photographs of the Vermont State Fair by Jack Delano. One of them shows a sideshow barker drinking from a soda bottle. The pictures show the signs stating that the Longest Snake was in the tent. There is also Teddy the Wrestling Bear. The photos are from 1941. The placard states that these were recent prints made from the original negatives.

Manny: Wait. I'm confused. Is this an original picture or a copy?

Sid: It's both, I guess.

Manny: That makes no sense.

Sid: Sure it does. What we are looking at is a new picture. But how was the picture made? Through the old negative. The negative is the old art. But we can't see a negative, so we are looking at a new copy.

Manny: Yeah. I hear you. Still makes no sense. It's a copy and keep it at that.

Sid: Fine, it's a goddamn copy, but if there were no copy, we would be looking at a blank wall.

Manny: No we wouldn't. They would have put up something else. Maybe not as good a picture. But they got a lot of everything in the backroom.

Sid: What backroom?

Manny: The backroom. Every joint has a backroom. That's where all the old second rate stuff is kept. That's where all the costumes and empty beer bottles are kept.

Sid: And depression era photographs?

Manny: No doubt. They got to be kept somewhere.

Sid: I like this photo. It's really great.

Manny: I ain't saying it ain't. I'm just saying that it kind of isn't original art.

Sid: Who cares? I mean look at that. That sign, Teddy the Wrestling Bear.

Manny: He'd be fake. A guy in a bear suit no doubt.

Sid: Who cares. People are paying a nickel to get in. And it ain't just a wrestling bear. There's the world's longest snake.

Manny: Fake.

Sid: Fake snake. Guy in a suit. Not an original copy of the photograph. You really are the worst person to take to the sideshow.

Manny: We ain't in a sideshow. We are in a museum.

Sid: You sure about that?

The boys look around and talk with an old guy who remembers going to the Vermont State Fairs back then, though he didn't remember the sideshow. He was just a little kid and his folks knew better than to have him go to the sideshow. We stop at a Dutch bakery a few miles away and have amazing sweets and good coffee. The boys both call the coffee decent, which is not a kind of compliment they give out easily.

New Britain Museum of American Art - New Britain Connecticut

August 26, 2018

Blame the lovely weather. We are the only ones in the museum for the first half hour. From the time it opens until 11:30, we see no one but the woman at the front desk and another at the gift shop. There are large spacious galleries with strong pieces on the wall. The boys have the whole place to themselves, and it unnerves them a little.

Sid: This is weird.

Manny: Nah, it's just an abstract piece. Kind of nice. It ain't weird.

Sid: That's not what I'm talking on. Asshole. No, I mean no one is here.

Manny: We're here.

Sid: No shit. I didn't know that. No I mean there are no guards in the gallery either. I'm sure there are cameras, but all the other places we've been, there's been guards too.

Manny: Yeah, true. I didn't realize. I knew it was quiet and all, but I didn't even notice them not there.

Sid: Well, there was that one guard.

Manny: What guard?

Sid: The guard. That old guy. With his arms crossed.

Manny: By the door to the first gallery?

Sid: Yeah, the old guy, dumb look on his face.

Manny: The guy that didn't move one bit?

Sid: Yeah.

Manny: The guard that was a statue?

Sid: What the fuck? It was a guy.

Manny: It was a lifelike statue.

Sid: Bullshit, it looked like a guy.

Manny: Yeah, sure.

Sid: I even said hi to him when I passed by.

Manny: Yeah, sure.

Sid: Oh, fuck me. I was even a little pissed at him that he didn't say hi back.

Let me stop the boys here. What they saw was a statue called Security Guard by Mark Sijan. The statue is amazingly lifelike. It stands before the first door with his arms crossed and slightly bored and slightly amused expression on his face. The piece must have gotten a lot of people poking it, because there is a sign behind it that reads, "Please do not disturb the concentration of the security staff by touching him. Thank you."

Manny: So there are no guards in this whole place. Well, ones that ain't art.

Sid: I don't appreciate art that pretends to be law enforcement.

Manny: So what do you like your art to pretend to be?

Sid: Look, art shouldn't fool a guy? That shit is not acceptable. Art should look like art. Hanging on a wall, with a fucking frame. They should know that this is art and this a bored guy who ain't moving, not because he's made of plastic, but because he has learned the art of not moving. Art of not moving. Not a piece of art itself.

Manny: You sound pissed off, like someone swindled you Sid.

Sid: Fuck yeah I've been swindled. I talked to a piece of fucking art. Excuse my English, but that fucking sucks. Art. Fooling a fella. That shit ain't what art is supposed to do.

Manny: What is art supposed to do?

Sid: Wipe that fucking smile off your face and I'll tell you. Art is for looking at and thinking about the things in the world.

Manny: And one of the things in the world is getting played. You was.

Sid: Not one bit. That's bullshit is what that is. I bet that every now and then they get a real person to impersonate the security guard statue, a guy who can stay really still. I bet they do this just to fuck with the museum goer's head. They will never know if what they're seeing is real or not.

Manny: What a lame ass excuse. That's bullshit. I bet you they already changed up the guy with the statue downstairs and when we go down you will be able to tell it's art and not a guy.

Sid: No doubt, museums are fucking sneaky like that.

With more grousing, they finish looking around and then go across the street to walk in the Walnut Hill Park. They see a bunch of men setting up a game of cricket. The boys knew they would not be able to understand it and left. They find a nice restaurant pub that was opening up it's door. They figured this was something easy to understand and ordered accordingly.

Schiltkamp Gallery at Clark University. Worcester Massachusetts. Likeness Exhibition.

September 16, 2018

The boys are shocked to discover that there was a gallery in town that they didn't know about. Better than that, this gallery shared a parking lot with Flying Dreams Brewing Company. To them, this was what art was all about and they were in good spirits, which, I must say, is very similar to them in a shitty mood. The space has a bored undergraduate manning the table, watching sitcoms on her computer, and a nice show of contemporary portraits. There is a good amount of photographs and drawings. The one the boys focus on are a series of self portrait photographs by Caleb Cole. Cole cast himself in a variety of environments and costumes. He is dressed as a housewife in one, as a sailor in another, as a woman in a black leather dress while holding a whisk. They remind me of what Cindy Sherman used to do. I don't mention that to the boys, because they really would not have cared. I can hear them, and some of you, say, "Cindy-fucking-who?"

Manny: So the guy in the pictures. With the sideburns. That guy. Is he the photographer?

Sid: Yeah, these are self portraits.

Manny: And he's saying something about the inner self of these people he's pretending to be.

Sid: If you say so. I don't know about inner self. I try to avoid inner self.

Manny: Don't we all. Is it just me, but are you sick of the artists drawing and photographing themselves?

Sid: The selfie effect.

Manny: No, it's not a selfie. It's sitting down and thinking to yourself, I want to make me some art. I want to get in a gallery show with the art I'm going to be making and now, what should the subject be? Why me, of course. I'm the best subject for art. A selfie is just a snapshot. A boring ass snapshot, but still just a pic. Self portraits, that's saying that I am the center of art.

Sid: No it's not. It's just thinking to yourself, I ain't got money to pay a model, I might as well do it myself.

Manny: Maybe so, for some. But you know that there are some artists who don't ask, what is the subject of my art, but instead they ask what weird scenarios am I going to put myself into this time.

Sid: Are you saying artists are self involved assholes?

Manny: No, I am not saying artists as a class are self involved assholes, but I am saying that there is a subset of them who are self involved assholes.

Sid: I kind of like these photos. They got a theme going on. They're sad. I can spend some time trying to figure out what the character in the shot is thinking. Like, why does he, when he's in that hot girl dress, have a whisk in his hand? I've been puzzling over that one.

Manny: No, I ain't complaining about these, I can handle these. I'm just seeing a lot of artists putting themselves in frames and I got to ask, is that the only topic you can think of?

Sid: Back to selfies with that question. Everyone can take pictures now with their phones. They take pictures of themselves. Boring choices. At least the artists can do something more than making duck lips at the camera.

We get as much out of the gallery as we can and then head across the parking lot to Peppercorns, which houses the Flying Dreams Brewery. There is a good amount to sample and the boys are happy drinking their beer and looking at themselves in the bar mirror.

Thorne-Sagendorf Art Gallery, Keene State College, Keene, New Hampshire. Mark Hogancamp: Women of Marwencol and Other Possible Histories

September 22, 2018

As the information on the sign says, the artist started this project after being a victim of a violent assault. As part of therapy, he made dioramas and ⅙ scale figures. He created a world called Marwencol. They kind of feel like old school G.I. Joe from the sixties to me, not that I am old enough to remember that, but I have seen the old ads and that's what this reminds me of. In the gallery are a variety of photos he made of the models. They have spy women and men soldiers doing something important. My favorite is the motorcycle women models around male soldier models. It is unreal and very compelling. The boys smile throughout. They start remembering all the old war movies and TV shows that this remind them of.

Sid: This is great. This is like kid play, making stories with action dolls but it's grown up and then he took pictures of it to show to his friends. This is art? Well if this guy fooled the art snobs, more power to the guy.

Manny: Yeah, I like it, it's cool.

Sid: Ah man, I hear a but coming on.

Manny: Because there's a but coming on.

Sid: I fucking knew it.

Manny: I think it's great, but I wish they didn't have to mention that the guy, the artist, was hurt in an attack.

Sid: Well he was, so why shouldn't they mention it?

Manny: Because that's not the art. The art is the art. It's not the attack or whatever happened to him. The art doesn't have to stand on a guy getting beat down.

Sid: But the beat down happened. It made him want to do something, he made this.

Manny: So is this just fucking therapy? Are we looking at therapy? Are you liking it because the guy made good breakthroughs in his session that day?

Sid: Jesus. Relax. He made art. I get it. I like it. It's like toy commercials but more than that. And I don't mind knowing why he started doing.

Manny: And would you like it if you didn't know about what started it?

Sid: Yeah, I well, yeah. The shit's okay.

Manny: So why know about it? It doesn't change whether the stuff is liked or not, so why say anything at all?

Sid: I don't know, maybe some people will like it more because of knowing.

Manny: Then they're assholes and they shouldn't see the art.

Sid: You want to stop people from looking at art if they want to know why the art was made?

Manny: Yeah, like the art or get the fuck out. Parking is hard enough without assholes looking for a sob story with their art watching.

Sid: Only asshole here is you.

Manny: Fair enough, but I'm one of the good assholes. I mean I'm looking at the art to look at art. I'm not looking at the art because someone got hit or had cancer or was sad that day.

SId: Know about it or not know about it, the art is here. Might as well know about it.

Manny: Why? So you can feel more? Then he should put it in the art and not in the bio.

Sid: Damn. Imagine if you didn't like the art.

Manny: If I didn't like the art, I wouldn't say jack shit. Not worth the time. Too much bad shit out there. I only complain about the shit I like.

Sid: You must like a lot then.

Manny: Enough.

They go into the another part of the gallery and see a show about adolescence and didn't have anything to say, positive or negative. After that, they enter into the gallery's Andy Warhol exhibit

Thorne-Sagendorf Art Gallery, Keene State College, Keene, New Hampshire. Andy Warhol

September 22, 2018

The show is photographs from the Factory period for Warhol. It includes some information letting us know that the Warhol Foundation gifted fifty small museums in fifty states art and ephemera from the Warhol collection as part of the Andy Warhol Photographic Legacy Project. The sign in the gallery mentions that most of the photographs were taken by Stephen Shore. The boys read this and are confused.

Manny: Wait, hold the fuck on. Is this a Stephen Shore show or an Andy Warhol show?

Sid: Read the title of the gallery, asshole. Andy Warhol.

Manny: But why does this say the guy taking all these photographs is Stephen Shore? What the fuck.

Sid: Because no one gives a shit about Stephen Shore. People care about Andy Warhol.

Manny: Lots of people care about Stephen Shore.

Sid: Who?

Manny: I don't fucking know. I don't know the guy. But I'm sure his folks know him. His people care. They must be pissed that Stephen Shore gets second banana status on his own photographs.

Sid: The hell he is. His name is up there in the sign. It's Stephen Shore's work.

Manny: The hell it is. What fucking exhibit are we in right now?

Sid: It's an Andy Warhol show.

Manny: Andy Warhol show. That's right. That's goddam right. The guy who took the pictures is only mentioned in one placard sign. You got to search for his name. But Andy Warhol, he's big and large and not the guy who took the fucking pictures.

Sid: The guy with the name is the guy who gets people to come look.

Manny: That's bullshit, the guy who makes the art, who takes the pictures of the people dancing or whatever, that's the guy who gets the people to come look. What the fuck, is Andy Warhol the producer? Is he the ringmaster of the circus?

Sid: Look at these pictures, that's not far from what I'm seeing.

Manny: And the only reason you are seeing it is because fucking Stephen Shore took the pictures.

Sid: No. The only reason we are seeing these pictures right now is that they were held onto by Andy Warhol. If it wasn't for him and his big fucking name, then no one would have held onto these photos and no one would have sent them to Keene fucking New Hampshire and no one would be bitching and moaning about who the real artist is.

Manny: So we all owe a debt of gratitude to Andy Warhol?

Sid: I don't owe shit to Andy Warhol. But Stephen Shore would not be someone we would be arguing about if it wasn't for Andy Warhol.

Manny: He should be bigger in the sign. He should be getting credit.

Sid: But we are talking about him for like ten fucking minutes. Isn't that enough? We're looking at his images. We are talking about his worth. Ain't that enough?

Manny: I worry about all the artists who did the work. Maybe the ones we don't know the names of.

Sid: I worry that this fucking conversation is never going to end.

We leave there and a good deal of time getting lost on the campus. We eat at a Rasmussen Pizza, and Sid asks Mannyt if he is worried that someone other than Rasmussen was making his pizza and Manny tells him to fuck off.

Yale Gallery of Art - Modigliani's Portrait of a Young Woman
September 29, 2018

I have always admired the boys' ability to not give a shit about being in an art museum or gallery. They come in their work boots and their flannel shirts and they talk like they talk and never seem to be fazed with the difference between them and everyone else present. It's a skill, or it's dumb blind ambivalence, I am not quite sure which. But here, in the heart of Yale, they seemed uncomfortable. It is very impressive just being in this slice of New Haven. And the gallery itself, all four floors of it, is imposing. To add to the pressure, there is another Yale Museum of Art right across the street, that one devoted to nothing but British art. The boys vetoe that destination. "The hell with Limey art. Let's stick to USA art." With that said, they stop and look at a Modigliani, an Italian artist. The painting is lovely. It has the long neck that people associate with Modigliani, but it is unique in that it is a painting of a head in profile. The long nose is also a major feature of the work. I'm pleased that they stopped and looked at this particular painting, because if I was just by myself, this would be the painting I would stop and stare at.

Manny: I knew a girl who looked just like that.

Sid: No you didn't, shut up.

Manny: What? I ain't supposed to be true here? I knew a girl who looked like that. A perfect goddam copy.

Sid: No, this ain't a, whatsitcalled, a realistic representation. This is not real.

Manny: Then you didn't know Jenny McNamara.

Sid: Who the hell is Jenny McNamara?

Manny: Jenny McNamara, she's the girl in the picture.

Sid: No, that ain't who the guy painted. Look at the sign. It don't say Jenny McNamara. It says Portrait of a Young Woman.

Manny: Yeah, and Jenny McNamara was a young woman. Well, she ain't now. She's my age and I guess she's still around. I wonder if she's still around. Her family moved after sixth grade and to be true, I haven't thought a moment about her until I saw her in the painting here today.

Sid: You still never seen her today. You see a picture that has nothing to do with her. It was done, look at that, it was done a hundred years ago, exactly.

Manny: That can't be, because Jenny McNamara ain't that old. She was mature for her years. Sure. She was smart and didn't take guff from me or no one. But she is not a hundred years old.

Sid: And she still ain't. She's a girl and this is a painting.

Manny: But it's her alright. I wasn't sure at first but damn, look at that nose. Only Jenny McNamara had a nose like that.

Sid: No one had a nose like that. Ever. That's the artist making a point. It's like the neck, no one has a neck that long.

Manny: Jenny McNamara had a neck that long.

Sid: It's the artist doing the artist thing. It has nothing to do with real anatomy.

Manny: Don't talk like that to Jenny McNamara. She is kind of sensitive.

SId: It's not her.

Manny: Of course it is. It has to be. I see her. I believe it's her. I wish she didn't move away. I kind of liked her a lot. This painting. This gets it fine. She's there.

Sid: Shit. I take it you really like this painting.

Manny: Oh come on. I wouldn't go that far.

As we head out and Sid goes to the Men's Room, I see Manny quickly find and purchase a postcard of the Modigliani and then slip it in his back pocket. I am sure it is well bent and wrinkled by the time we find a drinking establishment that doesn't feel too good for them. They have to walk well past the college to find a bar that feels like a bar and not like a learning moment with alcohol.

The University of Saint Joseph Art Museum, West Hartford, Ct. In Memoriam: Commemorative Works by Contemporary Artists

October 4, 2018

I really should steer them to museums in Catholic schools more often. The boys are very aware of their environment and don't swear once. I am not sure who I had with me. The museum is very small, just six rooms, and all they do is exhibitions. That's alright, because the show knocks the boys out a little bit. The concept is that all of the art is in memory of a loved one or in honor of a disaster. The work has power. The one that stops them from walking is a red plush sofa that is tilted forward so that we can see both the back and the seat of the couch. Running the length of the cushions is embroidered lettering. The words are in Spanish but the sign has the translation. The words (I'm not going to write them here) are the words of a suicide note from a mother to her daughters, hoping they will forgive her. The piece is called "A mis adorables hijas" which translates as "To My Adorable Daughters." The sign explains that the artist, Pepon Osorio, was inspired to do this from a real story where a woman killed herself and left her note pinned to the cushion of her red plush sofa. The artist made the sofa the suicide note.

Sid: I don't like it.

Manny: Pretty powerful.

Sid: I know, and that's why I don't like it. It's too powerful for its own good.

Manny: I don't get you.

Sid: I mean, the words, the words written on it, are they the real words?

Manny: They're real words, just in Spanish. But they're real.

Sid: No you son of a. I mean no. I mean this is based on a real suicide. The note was pinned to a couch. Are these words the real words to the note? The note the real woman wrote?

Manny: Wait, Okay. Are those a real suicide note words? Let me check. I don't know. It ain't clear. I think he was inspired by it so maybe he made up the words.

Sid: He better have. I don't like it if he just used the real words.

Manny: But doesn't that make it powerful? Real? The real words. The real goodbye as part of the sofa. That's some heavy stuff.

Sid: No. That's pornography.

Manny: I don't see no dirty pictures. This ain't pornography.

Sid: It don't get any dirtier than using the words of a suicide note for art. That's porno. That's obscene.

Manny: Still, it's just a couch with some words written on it. Words we can't read without a translation on the sign.

Sid: These are the words the daughters read when they came down and found the note. And now someone is making art from it. How much dirtier and wrong does something have to be to be called obscene?

Manny: Let me look at the sign. Like I said, I'm not sure but it seems like he based it on a news story. So he probably didn't have the note from the newspaper story. They don't reprint those. So you can cool off a little. It seems like the artist made up the words.

Sid: Good, but that ain't much better.

Manny: I give up, what are you upset with now? The suicide note sofa isn't real.

Sid: Then the artist had to pretend and make up the suicide note. He had to think of what it could be. That's messed up. It came out so well. Like it was easy for us to make up suicide notes. No, I ain't feeling any better about this art.

Manny: Art aint supposed to make you feel better. It's just supposed to make you feel, dummy.

Sid: Then it worked. It did its job.

Manny: Yeah, it's heavy stuff. It did its job.

Sid: I still don't like it.

Manny: Me neither.

They look at the other art. One of them has Godzilla in the art and that makes Sid pretty happy. He has a soft spot for Godzilla. Then he is back to the sofa piece and staring at it, shaking his head slowly. They tell me it is time to go and we find a place called New Park Brewery. The beer is cold and the boys swear a lot, like they are making up for lost time.

New Hampshire Institute - Sharon Art Center Gallery, Peterborough, New Hampshire. Monadnock Art's Open Studio Tour Preview.

October 7, 2018

The next four chapters are all on the same day. It is a busy morning for the boys. The first stop is the Sharon Art Center Gallery where they are kicking off the annual open studio tour for over 40 artists in the area. Even just driving into town, we see several "Art Tour" signs with numbers on them, representing a stop we can make. The Art Center has a piece or two from each of the studios that might be visited. I think it a smart idea. You might see something and be intrigued and then plan to make a visit to that studio. Conversely, you can see something that doesn't charm you and you can cross that off the drive. There are the typical landscapes and fishing scenes, but also more adventurous paintings. There is glass work, ceramics and textile work. There is a felt turtle, looking happily green and cuddly. It is a wide and worthwhile selection.

Sid: Not a chance in hell.

Manny: Not a chance in hell, what?

Sid: Not a chance in hell that we are going to any of these studios. We are in the fucking art center, that's enough, ain't it?

Manny: Is it? This ain't really a show. This is more like paint swatches you pick up at Home Depot. It ain't a paint selection, it's the thing that helps you decide what paint to pick. You see the art here and you say, that's the one. Let's drive to that artist's house.

Sid: Bullshit on two counts. One, this is too an art show. There is art to say I like and I don't like. Just like all the other museums and galleries we done. No different, so don't think it isn't. And two, I don't want to go to no artist's studio.

Manny: This is a preview for the tour, ain't we taking the tour?

Sid: We certainly are not. Isn't it enough we are looking at art and thinking about art as much as we are? Now we have to go to their homes or their studios and look at the stuff with them there?

Manny: It's their place, where else should they be?

Sid: That's fine, but I don't have to go there. I don't want to go there. I look at the art. I've learned how to do that. I kind of like looking at the art. But talking to the artist while I'm looking at that art? That's a skill level I never want to fucking attain.

Manny: What? You tell them you like it and then eat the cheese and crackers they have out.

Sid: There's cheese?

Manny: Sometimes wine, I think.

Sid: No, not even for cheese and wine. That shit ain't worth it. Do we have to make small talk? Do we have to listen to them go on about their fucking process? I don't care about their process. I look at the art. That's my process and I'm fine with it.

Manny: I wouldn't mind talking to a few of the artists. I got to figure out what the hell they're thinking. Like that one. WIth the huge painting of the eyeballs. I got to talk to that guy and figure him out.

SId: And listen to him? There ain't enough cheddar cubes in the world to make me get through that.

Manny: So we are at the preview of a tour we won't go to?

Sid: We are at an art show and that's it. Art shows are us by ourselves looking at things. Not going to see their work in progress or compliment them. We look. We don't talk.

Manny: We don't?

Sid: To artists. We don't talk to artists.

Manny: Okay. Kind of blows the whole purpose of going to an art tour.

Sid: Look at the art that's here. There's a bar on the next block.

They talk about a few of the things they see and then leave, not to the Harlow, which is the name of the pub, but to a small museum on the next street called the Mariposa Museum & World Culture Center.

Mariposa Museum & World Culture Center. Peterborough, NH. "And Still We Rise: 44 Stunning Story Quilts Narrating 400 Years of the African American Experience." Satchel Paige by Edward Bostick.

October 7, 2018.

This is a lovely little museum that focuses on multicultural learning. The top floor has musical instruments from around the world and they encourage children (and grown-ups I suppose) to try them out. The quilt show is one of several exhibits. There are not 44 quilts, because half of the show is at the Canaan Street Meeting House in Canaan, New Hampshire. The story quilts do their job. They tell stories of struggle and of defeating racism. It's amazing what a square of cloth can tell. The boys stop in front of one, a portrait of an older African American man wearing a baseball cap.

Manny: Looks like a baseball player.

Sid: It's Satchel Paige.

Manny: From the Negro League.

Sid: He played MLB too. The Indians I think.

Manny: Only for a couple years, but yeah, he played MLB, but only got the chance in his forties for god's sake. Hell of a pitcher.

Sid: See him play much?

Manny: We say Babe Ruth was the best batter of all time. You see him play?

Sid: The quilt makes Paige look sad.

Manny: You be sad too if you put up with the shit he had to put up with.

Sid: The guy who made it, the quilter, he did a good job. That's a hell of a quilt. Which is something I don't think I ever said in my life.

Manny: It ain't a guy, right? It's a woman who made this.

Sid: You think guys can't quilt? And you call me old fashioned. I saw on a History Channel show that wounded British soldiers during Victorian times would make quilts as part of their recovery.

Manny: That's not what I meant, dick. Look at the sign for the exhibit. This is a show from the Women of Color Quilters Network. Well, look at the quilter's name

Sid: Edward Borwick.

Manny: Funny name for a woman.

Sid: So it's a guy.

Manny: This is put together by the Woman of Color Quilters. Shouldn't the quilts be done by a woman?

Sid: There's probably some rule or exception.

Manny: Not a woman.

Sid: Yeah, but it is talking about civil rights and shit, so it fits with the theme fine.

Manny: Not a woman.

Sid: You getting sexist on me? You getting a woman in the kitchen and the one to the knitting and the quilting? There can be only one useless shit in this partnership and that is still me.

Manny: And the crown is still yours, but damn, I'm just saying, if the group is women, then it should be women doing it. This is an art that is predominantly female, right?

Sid: Predominantly? Yeah, sure.

Manny: They made this a real thing. A real art. Hell, there are documentaries on Channel 2 talking about how it's an art and women, and women of color, made it that way.

Sid: Women of color. That's a fucking loaded throwback term.

Manny: Tell me about it, I feel weird saying it. Like someone is going to correct me. Like I'm going to correct me. Anyway, all I'm saying is that a guy shouldn't be in the show. Or if he has to be, he could have had a more non-specific first name, like Terry.

Sid: Fuck that, they picked it to be in the show cause it's good and he is one of the greatest pitchers of all time. It's Satchel Paige.

Manny: I see that

Sid: It's a good quilt.

Manny: Yeah, I know. I wouldn't be bitching about it if it wasn't.

With this small, but funky museum exhausted, we leave for the much anticipated beer at Harlow's.

Harlow's Pub, Peterborough New Hampshire. This is a discussion on "It's Five O'Clock Somewhere" Martini Glasses by Jordana Korsen. That was two chapters ago at the Sharon Arts Center. They only just now got around to talking about it.

October 7, 2018

The title kind of says everything I might say here in this paragraph. The boys went to a gallery and a museum in one morning. They deserved their beer. Harlow's has scores of beers on tap and this made all their art viewing worth it. The food was good as well. Manny had a roast beef sandwich with boursin cheese. He didn't know the cheese but he approved with the first bite. Sid had a tuna melt. Sid tends to have tuna melts. Now at these times, when they are drinking after the museums, the conversation is rarely about what they saw. They did their bit and they are done. But this was a little different. Something reminded Sid of a piece of art that he saw. It might have been the guy in the tweed jacket, down at the end of the bar, who ordered an extra dry martini. A bold choice for 11:30 on a Saturday morning. But if you need a stiff martini, then you need a stiff martini.

Sid: Martini glasses.

Manny: What about them?

Sid: They're a kind of fucked up design. With the long stem and the drink up to the edge. That shit is going to ripple and spill. That's a bad design.

Manny: If you spill your martini, it's a sign that you've had too many.

Sid: It's a lousy design.

Manny: Stick to beer.

Sid: And I am, but I was thinking about the whole thing when we was at the first place. The place that sets you off on the art tour that we ain't going on. Do you remember those glasses that was there?

Manny: Didn't I see like a hundred things today and it ain't noon?

Sid: Fair enough. There was this set of martini glasses, but instead of stems the bottoms are glass olives. The martini glasses are resting on giant, well balanced olives.

Manny: Yeah. I remember that. That was pretty funny. I liked those. So what's got you bout it?

Sid: Shit. I hate to say this. Because I feel like I'm always asking this same fucking question and I am sick of hearing me say it.

Manny: Let me guess, you going to ask, is it art?

Sid: Yeah, I want to know. Is it art?

Manny: Sure. Why not?

Sid: That's a bullshit answer.

Manny: What am I supposed to say? It is glassware and glassware cannot be art? Because it's the cocktail that's the fucking art and not the thing you slosh it into? Am I supposed to be saying that?

Sid: Yeah, You should be saying something like that, because it's true. I mean it's the container. The receptacle. Do we see packing crates as art? Paintings on the wall with frames and people talking about the frames and not about what it's surrounding

Manny: Why not? There was one of those snooty ass museums we went to early on, and I was thinking the art is crap but that frame has good word work and it had incredible aged color.

Sid: Great! Just fucking great. Now everything is art. The frame. The signs that describe the art. The way it is hung on the wall. All of it is now art.

Manny: What's the problem with that?

Sid: There has to be something that isn't art. If everything is art, nothing is art. Tell me, what isn't art in this day and age?

Manny: Parking tickets.

Sid: That's probably bullshit. There is an artist working their hardest transforming tickets into art. Performance art. Whatever the fuck that is.

Manny: Those martini glasses were funny. I liked them. They kind of would be the thing in a home bar in the 1960s. Kitschy. My dad would have liked it. He had a home bar and never used it. All he did was crack open cans of Gansett.

Sid: I just don't know if I would call it art. Is cool looking glasses art?

Manny: Why not? It might make someone happy to have them.

Sid: Is that what art is? It makes you happy?

Manny: Sure. That works.

They drink their beer. The art in the glass. And they noisily eat their sandwiches. They are the two loudest eaters I know.

The Emblem Museum. The Art of Julia Zanes. Brattleboro , Vermont

October 7, 2018

At the end of this long day of art watching, we drive to Brattleboro. The soul purpose is to see Manny's daughter, who has a cold. The visit is brief. On leaving town, Sid sees a sandwich board in front of a doorway on Elliot Street that states the second floor is the sight of the Emblem Museum. Sid swears and says, "Park the car. I never heard of it and we should do it. I can't believe I'm saying this, but let's fucking see more art." Upstairs are two rooms of paintings by one woman, Julia Zanes. There are allegorical paintings, as well as some beautiful abstracts. There is also a puppet theater and an amazing sculpture made of gold leaf. From behind a curtain, Julia Zanes appears. This is her studio, she explains, and she opens it up every Sunday for the public to see what she is working on. She shows us a puppet fortune telling machine. I put in four quarters, manipulate the puppet and get a fortune in a little plastic bubble container. I decide to not open it up until I really needed a fortune. Manny keeps on pestering me to look at it. Ms. Zanes says she is planning a puppet show for Halloween, she has a puppet stage after all, but has not figured out what to do. We compliment her for letting us see her work and wish her well. We get in the car and I point us back to Massachusetts. For the first five minutes in the car, Manny keeps on laughing quietly to himself.

Sid: Okay, okay. What is so fucking funny.

    Manny: The Emblem Museum.

    Sid: That ain't right. She was nice. The art was alright, not my thing, but alright. So why you laughing at it?

Manny: I'm laughing at it because it ain't a museum.

Sid: She called it a museum.

Manny: But it's only her work. And she only opens it up when she is there. And she paints in the front room. You know what that sounds like? It sounds like it's her studio.

Sid: Fine. It's her studio.

Manny: And we went and had a studio tour. (Manny then peels out laughter.) You said, what? This morning that there was no way in hell you want to go to no artist's studio and here you are telling Dave to park the car to go to an open house art studio.

Sid: Fuck you.

Manny: Did your head explode? I even heard you talking to the artist. You complimented her. Oh. I fucking love it.

Sid: Shut up, Manny. I didn't know it was her studio.

Manny: I guess that's what artists need to do to get people to their studios. Call them museums.

Sid: Sure, why not.

Manny: Too funny.

We drive into Massachusetts and get home in under two hours. Sid is quieter than usual. But he is probably tired from the long day.

The Portsmouth Athenaeum. Portsmouth, New Hampshire. Painting Portsmouth Notables 1750-1850.

October 20, 2018

It is a beautiful day and the sidewalks are crowded. We see a sign for the Athenaeum which is featuring an exhibit and the boys don't say anything. They just turn to the open door and head up. They know that if there is art to see, they are going to see it. After nearly a year, they are getting pretty well trained. Even if it is to be a historical art exhibit. We trudge up three flights to get to the site. They have long tables and people going through genealogy. To the right is the exhibit gallery. There are portraits of stiff looking men. All the men look constipated. There are a few portraits of young women with small knowing smiles, like they are in on the joke. Whatever the joke might be. The boys are fascinated by a display of silhouette profiles. They want to talk their talk about it, but stop each other, glancing over at the ancient little old docent lady. She is not five feet from them, blithely smiling. She says she is happy to have us appreciating the history and the art of Portsmouth. The boys, of course, want to do their thing, talk their talk. They just can't do it. Sid point at the silhouette profiles and says, "Hold that thought." Then they march down the stairs and walk a block to the Thirsty Moose Taphouse. The bar has taps and taps of hundred of beers. They both get a local, Smuttynose Beer and let loose. They do not like their conversations interrupted. They down two pints of the brew each before speaking a word to each other. Then they begin.

Manny: Everyone was fucking miserable two hundred years ago.

Sid: Everyone was fucking miserable two hundred minutes ago. So what?

Manny: Fuck you, I'm talking art, not common misery. Everybody is fucking miserable, no doubt, but to look at all the fucking selfies in the world, no one would know it.

Sid: Selfies ain't art, they're just pictures to send to friends.

Manny: And that's what those big ass portraits in that place we was at are, they're slow drying selfies.

Sid: What the fuck. They are portraits to put on the wall. Not selfies.

Manny: Same purpose though. To hang in your own place so that friends will see it and go, damn, that's a great picture.

Sid: No one in 1805 Portsmouth ever said that.

Manny: I know you're old Sid, but I didn't know you went back that far.

Sid: You know what I mean, and by the way, fuck you.

Manny: They look severe and wooden in those poses because that's what was cool back then. They were able to smile and relax their shoulders, sure, but that wasn't what everyone was doing. Just like selfies. No one in real life makes that fish face they all do, but it's the thing.

Sid: Okay, if there was selfies for the colonies it was those silhouettes. You know, the ones we was looking at in the case in the middle of the room.

Manny: How is that selfies?

Sid: Well it was cheaper. What the thing say, it was like twenty five cents to get one made. That's closer to simple pictures.

Manny: It wasn't our quarters. Quarter had to be serious fucking money.

Sid: Sure, but how much, five bucks? Ten bucks? Still pretty fucking cheap.

They lose the conversation somewhere along the line and just stare at their phones. I catch both of them going through the pictures they took, swiping through them while drinking their beers. It is quiet for them, with them thinking thoughts about art and photographs that they decide to not share.

Fitchburg Art Museum. Fitchburg, Massachusetts. Interior Effects: Furniture in Contemporary Art.

November 3rd, 2018

The museum is loud and more crowded than usual. When we arrive, an awards ceremony for high school artists is just finishing up and all the young artists and their families are milling about. The new show on the second floor is on the use of furniture and how it can be made into art. The boys like the show more than they thought they could . They were sure they were going to bitch about sofa as modern art and what a bullshit idea that was (their words, not mine.) They are surprised by the humor and the variety of what is here. Some of it is well made furniture, some of it is sculpture using or commenting on furniture. Either way, the boys like it. It turns out, there favorite two pieces are both by the same artist: Liz Shepherd. The first, Untitled (Blue), is a blue dresser cut in two and the clothes are falling out. The second one are large silk screened full sized pictures of furniture put onto plywood and placed on a wall. It is a large wall of floating seventies style couches and lazy boys. The boys both comment how fun these two are. And then Manny steps back and read the placard describing the work.

Manny: What the hell.

Sid: What, what the hell?

Manny: Listen. "Shepherd has frequently used furniture in her printmaking, sculpture and installation as a metaphor for loss and displacement."

Sid: What? Loss and what?

Manny: That's what it says. I can read it again.

Sid: Don't fucking bother. It won't make any more sense the second time. We are talking about the wall of floating sofas?

Manny: Yeah, and the cut in half chest of drawers. That one too.

Sid: I like those two pieces.

Manny: I like them too.

Sid: They're fun.

Manny: Yeah, they're fun. Colorful too.

Sid: And what the hell are they metaphors for?

Manny: Loss and displacement.

Sid: How? No. Stop. Why?

Manny: Hold on, let me check. Okay, the first one, the cut in two dresser, that is, wait, here it is, "The frissure through the center of this found dresser suggest the emotional impact of change or separation."

Sid: It does?

Manny: It says so here.

Sid: And the floating furniture. What the fuck deep meaning does that one have?

Manny: Hold on, let me check. Okay, hold on. It goes, "Shepherd based her wall-mounted silkscreen plywood couches, chairs and ottomans on the Company's iconic New England designs, considering the way colors, patterns and furniture have been advertised as male or female based on cultural norms."

Sid: So these pictures of furniture on the wall is supposed to be about gender?

Manny: Yeah. The sign says, yeah. It's about how they used to sell certain pieces by gender. That's the thing.

Sid: I don't see that at all.

Manny: Me neither.

Sid: Am I supposed to see serious shit about men and women in this? I just see furniture.

Manny: Floating furniture

Sid: Colorful fucking furniture.

Manny: Can I say, I like it? Not in a serious way? In a, this shit is pretty cool, way?

Sid: For fucking once, we are in agreement. So did the artist write that shit, what you read, or did the museum figure that everything had to be damned serious?

Manny: I don't see nothing that makes it clear. I don't know. If I had to guess, I bet you this was a consensus. Both sides agreed to this.

Sid: Some agreement. Here's the thing, shit like that makes me question if I am looking at the art the right way. Now if that's what the art is about, that's what the art is about. Art is serious shit and if you got to be angry or pissed to make it, so be it. Now me, I see something fun and cool, like the cut in two dresser, and I say, that's fucking cool. And that's it. I am not looking at separation and sadness. Now I got to ask, am I looking wrong? Because I don't have a fucking theory, am I allowed to like or not like art?

Manny: I say yeah. I say we are allowed to like shit without the artist statement. Just that we probably should keep that shit to ourselves. God knows what museum people think of people who say the art is cool.

Sid: Take away our art looking privileges.

Manny: No doubt.

They keep their mouths and their opinions to themselves for the rest of their time here. They go to the River Styx Brewing Company. It is a good time, but Manny won't stop singing that Blue Oyster Cult Song. "Don't Pay the Ferryman, till he gets you to the other side."

Spaightwood Galleries. Upton, Massachusetts. A Miro Show Going up while a Pierre Alechinsky show is being taken down

November 10, 2018

This one was my call. There are not a lot of professional retail galleries in Central Massachusetts. They tend to be in Boston or the other major hubs in New England. Worcester has scarcely any galleries and places showing art for sale. I mean, sure there is the bookstore or the coffee shop with art on the wall that you can buy if anyone working there knows how much to sell it for. But not galleries like in Newbery Street or anywhere in Downtown New York. This part of New England is dry. I heard of this place, where a retired couple from the Midwest bought an old church and renovated it into a gallery for modern art. I was told there was a lot of prints I would not be able to afford. So what else is new? I told the boys to shut up and just go where I took them. A year of shepherding the two of them in and around art has made me a little tougher than when I started. The place is beautiful and shaggy. The walls are filled with amazing art, most of it abstract. The center of the church has storage tables with boxes filled with art. The counters are strewn with unframed art prints. There are bookshelves teeming with art books and exhibition catalogs all along the walls. There is art leaning against bookshelves. There is art on other art. There is a ladder near a rare blank patch of wall that will no doubt have art covering it in the near future. An old man enters from a back room and introduces himself as the owner. He speaks to me and Manny for our time here. He is so enthusiastic about the artists he loves. He says this is the largest art gallery in New England in regard to quantity of art for sale. "I would love to not sell anything, but the IRS doesn't like it when I don't sell the art." He speaks of Miro and

Alechinsky and Chagall and Lichenstein and Joan Mitchell and artists I never heard of before. Andy, the owner, says he has more art than can be framed and he reuses the frames depending on what type of artist he wants to see on the walls. Sid, as we know, hates talking to others about the art, so he walks around, making sure to be on the opposite side of the gallery from where we are. We leave and drive to a nearby restaurant in Mendon, Willow Brook Restaurant, with a bright comfortable bar area. The boys drink domestic and eat quesadillas.

Manny: That was a nice guy, the owner of that joint.

Sid: That was a crazed art freak.

Manny: Sure, he was a nice crazed art freak. Who else would surround themselves with so much art?

Sid: He talked a lot about Miro, like we were supposed to know his different phases and different goddam whims.

Manny: I thought you weren't part of the conversation, not even introducing yourself to the guy.

Sid: Sound fucking travels. We were the only people in the place, I could hear everything, I just didn't want to talk about the art. I wanted to look at it and get the hell out of there, like we do.

Manny: I could have stayed a little longer. There was a lot of shit all over the place to look at.

Sid: I ain't saying that it was bad, it had more good art than a lot of the museums we been at. Of course that's just a volume game. He had a lot of art all over the place. There was bad art sure, but there was a lot of everything and some of the stuff had great colors.

Manny: Did you hear what he was saying about finding art he lost?

Sid: Must have blocked the sound out there.

Manny: He was saying how he was taking down the, what was his name, Alechinsky or something, his art. His show is over and he was putting up Miro and he was taking one of the Miro prints out of the frame and like fucking that, there was another Miro print behind it in the frame. He didn't know it was there. He was wondering where that print was, now he knew. That thing was behind that other print for like fucking years. For years. I looked at the tag, this was like a three thousand dollar thing. And he was just like, oh, there it is. Just like that. He said he also found these other prints from this other artist underneath some shit. Didn't know where these were like for fucking ever.

Sid: No way to run a gallery.

Manny: Said he and his wife been at this joint running it for like fifteen years or something like that.

Sid: Beginners luck.

Manny: Yeah bullshit. The place had art I wasn't that interested in and I was looking at some of the small Miros going, and thinking I maybe can swing that. That would look good in the back room.

Sid: You got fuck all up in the walls in your back room. Anything would look good up there.

Manny: But this was nice. I'm thinking about it. I'm thinking about the blue and the shape. Ain't that the shit? I'm thinking about art like I want to keep it.

Sid: Art ain't for owning. It ain't for investing. It's for looking at.

Manny: Yeah. And if it was in my back room I would be looking at it. That's how that shit works.

Sid: No, haven't you been paying attention. We going all the fucking time and haven't you been paying attention. You look at it on a wall. In a museum. In a gallery if you're stuck. You look at it and you move on. You might want to buy the postcard in the gift shop, but that's as far as you should go.

Manny: Why? People buy art all the time. They buy art because they like it. They buy it because they want to show off how fucking rich they are. Millions of dollars for an Andy Warhol.

Sid: That's bullshit. Millions of dollars for that shit. Crazy rich assholes. Let the art stay in the museums. All this shit about how much this is worth and how much that is worth.

Manny: I aint wanting a million dollar piece of shit. I was just thinking about one of those Miro prints. I like the color.

Sid: And that's how it starts.

Manny: Nothing is starting. I'm just thinking. I mean, shit, I am having a four thousand dollar thought. It's probably going to stay at that.

Sid: They say if you can't get a piece of art out of your head, you have to buy it. And just like that. You are a fucking art collector.

Manny: We go to museums almost every week.

Sid: But we ain't taking the paintings home with us.

Manny: No, because that would be fucking art theft.

Sid: That it would be.

Manny: I like the art we saw. I'm thinking about one of them. I can keep it just to that. Wouldn't be a bad thing to go back. I wouldn't mind taking my daughter to the place. She might think its a hoot.

Sid: You buy a Miro, I won't know what to say.

Manny: I know what you would say. And fuck you too.

Sid: Drink your beer.

Manny: Sure.

They have a few more beers and, realizing they devoured the quesadillas, order the mozzarella sticks, which are pretty good.

Worcester Art Museum, Worcester Massachusetts, Rediscovering Brilliance
December 8, 2018

In a small gallery at the Museum, there is on display large, bright religious stained glass. The sign for this explains that a church in Boston around 1899 had these made from the Tiffany company. The church closed in 1975 and they boxed up the Tiffany windows and donated them to the Worcester Art Museum. The boxes were never opened until 2016 and then they were restored and now here they are. They are beautiful, in a serious Bible Stories for All sort of way. One of them is an angel bending down, touching its reflection in water, creating a stunning effect.

Sid: That sucks.

Manny: It's windows with angels, it doesn't suck, but I do feel like I'm eight years old again and I'm not paying attention to the priest and my old man is going to swak me for it.

Sid: No, I mean it sucks that no one has seen these for like, what, like for forty years. Forty goddam years. This is Tiffany and that's a name that people like to see. And they was in boxes. For forty years. Some old folk probably were thinking of the windows they saw every Sunday and wondered, where are they, I wouldn't mind looking at those angels again and can they? No, they're in boxes in Worcester.

Manny: Do you really think there were some old eighty year olds missing these? Jonesing to see them after all those years?

Sid: Sure I do. They looked at these things for decades. This was the art that was always with them. It's the art in their church. When they was bored they looked at the cute angel. That's the art that you don't think about until you are old, and you go, you know I looked at Tiffany glass every week of my life, I wouldn't mind looking at it again.

Manny: Your old church ladies are much more interesting than any of my church ladies.

Sid: They do alright for themselves.

Manny: So it's a win, the old ladies who have lived can see it now, just have to take the train to Worcester.

Sid: That's likely, but it still sucks.

Manny: What sucks? Really? What sucks?

Sid: This is just one instant. This is just one thing in crates that made it out. How many more crates are down there?

Manny: Down where?

Sid: In the wherever they keep all the crates and the art they decide ain't good enough.

Manny: This is Tiffany, this stuff is good enough.

Sid: Tell that to all the mice running around the crates for forty years. They opened it up two years ago and realized what they had. What if the guy with the crowbar was sick that day? What if they walked by it and opened up something else and got something that wasn't Tiffany stained glass? What if it was large paintings of dogs playing poker?

Manny: I like paintings of dogs playing poker.

Sid: Me too, all day. But that shit would never make it on the wall. I figure there are more crates of art than there is space to show them.

Manny: Yeah, that's the way it works.

Sid: But they don't do a good enough job. There is space and no art on it.

Manny: By the bathroom.

Sid: No, asshole. Didn't you notice the sign by the big exhibition room they got, the room for the big shows? There was a sign saying that the next show was going to be open in like two or three months. So that's a lot of real estate not doing jack. What about all the art in the warehouse, in the crates? How do you think they feel?

Manny: How does the canvas with paint on it feel? I won't even begin to know.

Sid: Can't they just throw some shit on the wall? Let us decide if we like it? They got all this art no one is seeing. Can't we just see some of it? I mean, what if its something we might like? Maybe it's something we would love. How the fuck would we know if we ain't ever going to see it?

Manny: I don't know. I guess it just depends on the guy with the crowbar and what he decides to open.

Sid: It's always up to the guy with the crowbar.

Manny: And that kind of sucks.

Sid: Like I was saying.

We wander around and decide on where to drink, which was the Boynton, but we stop and look at the photographs by the museum cafe.

Worcester Art Museum. Worcester, Massachusetts. Reflections by Tony King. December 8, 2018

The way out of the museum is to walk by the cafe, which at this hour, is empty. Manny notices the large black and white photographs of New England scenes and realizes that it is an art show. We walk around the empty tables checking out the pictures.

Manny: I guess this is what they do if they have too much art to show and not enough wall space. Put it in the restaurant.

Sid: And that sucks too.

Manny: Jesus, everything sucks for you lately. Art not on the walls but in crates sucks. Art on the walls but with tables around them, sucks.

Sid: It doesn't suck now, because there ain't no one eating here, but what if the place was packed? What if there was eaters all over the joint?

Manny: Then we wouldn't be going all around here. Don't want to be leaning in and around folk when they're trying to eat their overpriced Cobb Salad.

Sid: Yeah, so what if we came early and there were the red hat ladies slurping their soups. They are blocking us looking at the photos. Does that mean we are supposed to be rude ass bastards and push through anyway or is art not available to look at because it's brunch time?

Manny: We was talking about this already, there is only so many walls to put the art on. You got all this space, put some art up.

Sid: But if you are eating an overpriced sandwich, do you want someone right up against the table pondering the picture, going on about the chiaroscuro effect?

Manny: What the fuck is that?

Sid: I don't know, but I can tell you, I don't want to learn about it from a guy leaning next to me when I am trying to fucking eat.

Manny: Lots of coffee houses have art up on the wall for sale. Local artists a lot of the time.

Sid: That's a coffee house with people talking about the novel their gonna write or the band they wanna form. Who cares what's on the wall.

Manny: True.

Sid: The thing is, if there are tables near the paintings or photographs, I just can't accept it as art. I just see it as something that is hiding the holes in the wall.

They finish looking at the photographs, which are lovely, and then head to the Boynton. They sit at the bar and get Wormtown beer and a large order of steamers. They made a giant mess of eating it.

New England Quilt Museum. Lowell, Massachusetts. Liberty and Justice: The Satirical Art of Salley Mavor.

December 27, 2018

This is a beautiful building with the exhibition spaces upstairs. The boys didn't want to go to a "blanket museum" but I convinced them. The plan was to go to the Whistler House Museum, but it was closed for the holiday weekend. I am not quite sure why a museum would want to be closed during school vacation week, but here we are. We are in Lowell with no museum but the Quilt Museum. There are two main shows. They linger on this one that is not quilts but a video of little cloth dolls doing a version of Hansel and Gretel where the attack is on the President, Trump. It is a silent doll movie, but it made its points pretty well. It is colorful and mean, which is great for a doll movie making fun of the president. I realize I read about this show a few months before, because it was originally going to be presented at another venue, which then canceled the show because of the political nature. The Quilt Museum heard about the cancellation and put the show on. The part that is interesting to the boys is the glass display that holds a large amount of the sewn dolls, as well the props.

Manny: This is cool, right here. It's like the whole cast of the movie is here, hanging out, while we watch the flick.

Sid: They're puppets.

Manny: I think they're dolls. They got no strings and you can't shove a hand up them. Dolls.

Sid: Dolls then. They ain't actors. They're dolls.

Manny: But it was this little Trump doll that they filmed and you turn around and there's the film that he is in. I like it.

Sid: It's politics. I don't like politics in museums.

Manny: Bullshit, there is always politics in museums.

Sid: Name one.

Manny: There was that photo show about the people recovering from opiods that we saw in Brattleboro.

Sid: Drug crisis ain't politics.

Manny: It's ain't? Bullshit. It's all politics. Okay, so this is more in your face, but it's politics.

Sid: Keep it on YouTube, or on Saturday Night Live. Not in a museum.

Manny: Why?

Sid: Why?

Manny: Yeah, why can't political art be in a museum?

Sid: Because people might disagree with it.

Manny: Bullshit again. I disagree with a lot of the art I see. I don't say that I disagree with it. I just say what the fuck, I don't like it. And that's it. What's the difference between a political view I think is wrong and a shitty painting of a bunch of fruit I think is wrong?

Sid: That's not the same. You just walk away from the lousy painting.

Manny: So why can't you walk away from the lousy politics?

Sid: Art museums can't be like that. They should have shit everyone will want to see.

Manny: No. You were the one who told me about that museum that has a path for Muslims to avoid any painting of nudes so they won't be offended. Where was that?

Sid: Detroit. But they want the Muslims to see the art, and are just trying to be respectful.

Manny: And you can respectfully just shut the fuck up and walk by the things you don't like. That's a good way to be.

Sid: I think I want my politics in newspapers.

Manny: And that's your problem. No one reads newspapers. Let them see this and like it or not like it. Why not museums?

Sid: And these are not even quilts. This is a quilt museum and these are cloth dolls. Not quilts and political.

Manny: You got nothing.

Manny pushes him out of the space where the show is, saying "If you ain't going to like it, look at other things." They look at the other show, which is spectacular.

The New England Quilt Museum. Lowell, Massachusetts. The Fabric Collage Quilts of Susan Carlson.

December 27, 2018

This might not be clear in reading these pages, but the boys don't have conversations in front of everything they see. They are quiet for a lot of the exhibits and entire museums we have gone to. Sometimes it is because they didn't get anything from it, and have nothing to say. Other times, they are so happy and satisfied, the only thing they say is, "Good, right?" with the other replying, "Yeah, good." After looking at the political doll show at the Quilt Museum, they focus on the work by Susan Carlson, who created animals and portraits with amazing skill and color. I was blown away by what she did. There is a twenty foot quilt of a crocodile that made me gasp. So, I am surprised and a little disappointed that the boys kept mum throughout. I should have just been patient. We leave the museum after lingering in the gift shop, and find a place for lunch. We go to TreMonte Pizzeria. It is a classy kind of joint and I am happy they picked it. The food is good and the bar is excellent. The boys have gin and tonics, something I didn't know they liked. "It's a gin and tonic kind of day," one says to me. Then they start talking about Susan Carlson.

Sid: I thought those animal quilts were pretty alright. She was able to do stuff you couldn't do with paint or photos. That was like art that only a quilt could do. I was impressed. And that crocodile.

Manny: That was the shit.

Sid: But you know what was the thing that got me? All the other people looking at the quilts.

Manny: What? You were pissed that you didn't have the place to yourself?

Sid: No, asshole. It was nice to have folk at a museum. Sometimes it breaks me to think that only you and I are looking at the pictures, and that people who might really like this stuff ain't here.

Manny: So what about the people?

Sid: There were all women.

Manny: That's happened before.

Sid: Sure, but they were all talking to each other about what they saw. You didn't hear them?

Manny: I was being polite. Something everyone might try to do.

Sid: Fuck you. Yeah, I was listening. Why not. People listen to us when we go at it in galleries. So turnabout is fair play, you know. And they weren't talking like we talk about art.

Manny: Thank god for that.

Sid: No. Listen. They was all talking about technique. Like the way she made it. The use of colors, the choices, the use of pre-cut patterns over doing things free hand, whatever the fuck that all means. Everyone else there were all quilters too. In one room, a woman was talking about the artist's choices because she knew the artist.

Manny: So they are all quilters. Were they jealous or something? Were they talking smack about her, pissed that she made it to the big museum show and they haven't?

Sid: No, they were all cool with it. Impressed. I was thinking that it was kind of interesting to have all these women checking out their peer.

Manny: So does that mean this show was not for us? Because we don't quilt, we can't appreciate what we're looking at. No, you don't understand how brilliant this quilt is because you have never done it. Are we not allowed?

Sid: We're not allowed in most places we go to. Doesn't stop us though.

Manny: True.

Sid: I don't think that's it. I think it's great they all know what is going on. A real inside baseball kind of thing. But I liked the stuff. So it's fine. We can see it and not have to worry how she made it or why she chose that stitch and not another. Who gives a fuck. Just that we have always been the odd ones out at the museums. In this place, we were the odd ones out in a different way. That's all.

We have really good pizza and they got really drunk. It is a long drive home because Manny insists on singing all the Eagles songs he knows, which is the refrain to Life in the Fast Lane and all of Hotel California three times in a row. He even attempts to scat-sing the ending guitar solo. I think Sid is able to force himself to sleep throughout the performance.

Driving to the Addison Gallery of American Art. Philips Academy. Andover, Ma.

December 29, 2018

Though I have been there a good amount of time, I guess I forgot how to get to the place. I get off the roads to North Andover and not Andover. I am turning us around for a half hour, too proud to use my GPS. I keep on assuring the boys that I know where it is and using the phone is not necessary.

Manny: All this damned driving for a gallery. Is this trip worth going to see a small gallery?

Sid: I don't think this is a small gallery. I think it's a pretty decent sized museum.

Manny: So why's it called a gallery then?

Sid: The hell should I know. It's on the grounds of Philips Academy, they are all about the huge money and endowments. Maybe to a rich school it's too small to be a real museum. It's only ten thousand square feet or something, so to the rich that's just a gallery.

Manny: You don't know.

Sid: I just said I didn't know. I mean, this ain't a college, this is a private high school. And they got a museum on it? No high school should have a museum, right? So it's best call it a gallery. Don't intimidate the locals that way.

Manny: That's theory number two, you got any theories numbers three to seven?

Sid: Give me a minute.

Manny: So it's a rich school museum, is it free to get in?

Sid: Yeah, no fee. Rich kid school has its perks.

Manny: Yeah, to make us feel bad.

Sid: What?

Manny: They could charge us, you know like five bucks, but no, they make it free.

Sid: It's nice that it's free to see the art.

Manny: But they could have charged us a fiver. That way none of us lose face.

Sid: Who's losing face?

Manny: All of us. They got the guilt of being so wealthy they can run a museum and charge nothing. And we got the guilt because we are in the hands of the Man.

Sid: How?

Manny: They are showing off and we can do nothing but go see their great art collection, their wealth and say gee mister, thanks for letting me see your art for free.

Sid: It's a public service.

Manny: Bullshit it's a public service, it's them deigning to let us blue collars see their fancy wares.

Sid: Would you prefer that the art was in their mansions? In their storage facilities? Would you rather that you can only look at the pretty pictures in the coffee table books? Which you borrow for free from a library.

Manny: Better the art is to be seen. Better still, they try not to make us feel like worthless scum.

Sid: You can feel like worthless scum or not. You can see the art or not. All these places have a donation bin, put the fiver in if that makes you feel better, more upper class.

Manny: I can do that.

Sid: Free is good you know.

Manny: It's not free. I don't know where the hidden costs are. The bottom line under my feet. But I know it's there.

Sid: Paranoid son of a bitch.

Manny: Yeah, they haven't gotten me yet.

I finally find the right road to be on and we come up on Philips Academy. I then proceed to drive right by the entrance. The boys swear at me some more. I turn around and we finally park and get to the museum.

Addison Gallery of American Art. Philips Academy. Andover, Ma. Paul Manship and His Artistic Legacy.
December 29, 2018

This was a show celebrating one of the great sculptors that no one remembers, though everyone has seen. He made the Prometheus sculpture that's out in Rockefeller Center in New York. The main gallery has smaller, though similar, pieces that are fun to look at it. They have the sleak Art D'eco look. Manship has a large studio that they have turned into an artist's center. To celebrate this, the museum has four photographers go to the old studio and take photos and be inspired by what they saw. One of the artists is New England photographer Abelardo Morell. Instead of photographs, he used a 19th century technique where he painted on the photographic glass to make prints. What resulted are beautiful shapes that have a kaleidoscopic effect while still feeling like it is art deco or William Morris curtains. Morell used a computer to finish the images and then made prints. There is something quite lovely with the images and the fact that he used old and new technology.

Sid: These remind me of kaleidoscopes. Not the toy. The spy glass. Not that. They remind me of what you saw in it.

Manny: Yeah, you don't have to explain. I knew what you meant. The sign here said he made it to look kaleidoscopic, so I'm sorry, but you ain't coming up with an original idea.

Sid: Who wants original ideas? They always get you in trouble. You might as well take someone else's idea and just do it better.

Manny: That's a bad way of looking at artists being inspired by other artists. You really got a bad attitude about how art is made, ya know?

Sid: I got to tell you, my grandfather had a large Tiffany kaleidoscope. His boss gave it to him as a retirement present. Some people got watches when they was done working, he got a Tiffany kaleidoscope.

Manny: I don't get it, what's a Tiffany kaleidoscope.

Sid: It's a kaleidoscope, but made by Tiffany's. You know, the guys who made those stained glass windows we saw at the Worcester Museum, they also made kaleidoscopes. A little stained glass in a tube, I guess. The thing was good looking. LIke brass or something like it.

Manny: Tiffany made toys? Really?

Sid: My grandfather said it was Tiffany. You going to talk back to my grandfather?

Manny: Why are we talking about this thing your grandad had?

Sid: Because he allowed me to play with it when I did my chores. Not play. Look at for like two or three minutes. That's it. Couldn't get the thing dirty is what he said to me. And what I saw in the kaleidoscope is what I'm seeing in these. These things are like looking through my grandfather's prized possession.

Manny: What's here?

Sid: Yeah. Maybe nothing like it, but it's getting me to remember some shit I didn't know I knew. The part I loved about using it as a kid was slowly turning it, trying to get the right pattern, the right way for it to look. Then I'd stop and just look. Proud I got the pattern right.

Manny: What made the pattern right?

Sid: It looked right. Sometimes I couldn't get the right image, the way I wanted it to look and I would be pissed and my grandfather would give me shit and say it was a privilege to look through his kaleidoscope.

Manny: And these prints here remind you of that.

Sid: Yeah.

Manny: But that's not right, I mean you can't change these. It's the way the artist made them. It can't be turned and made into different patterns. When you were a kid, you were in control.

Sid: True, but who needs that. Being in control. Making the artistic choices. That's fucking exhausting. Let someone else turn the tube. Let someone else say when it's done. If I don't like it, I won't stop and look. If I like it, if it's right, I will stay and stare. Not for a long time, because, shit, we have places to be. Fair?

Manny: Fair.

The funny thing is, Sid doesn't have places to be. He just stays in that gallery room and looks at the prints. Manny gets bored and goes on and looks at the other exhibition, which is landscape photography. It is getting late and the guard informs us that the museum is closing in ten minutes. Sid nods and is ready to go. He is done. He says he is not thirsty or hungry and that we can wait until we got back to Worcester to stop for a drink. Manny's eyes get wide at this and just says, "If that's what you want." The ride is pretty painless and we go to VIncent's because the boys really want the meatball sandwiches they got there. They devour the sandwiches like they haven't eaten in weeks.

Afterword

And there it is. A year spent going to see art with two old pains in the asses. When I tell them that a year is a good amount of time to be driving them around, they agree.

"But we ain't done," Sid tells me.

"Yeah, we just started getting the hang of this art thing," Manny says.

"Wait, you want to keep doing this?" I ask.

When they say they do, I discover I am pleased to hear it.

Description

Sid and Manny are two retired guys who decide to go to art museums and galleries, to see what there is to see. This is their hobby. They look at art and crafts and talk to each other about what the art. They don't talk quietly and politely, but are you going to tell them to pipe down?

Join the two as they spend a year looking and talking about art in New England. They saw a lot of art in 2018, and this is your chance to listen in on their views.

Art in New England (with Sid and Manny) is an irreverent and witty look at art and the act of going out and viewing the art.

About the Author

David is putting out as many short little books as he can. He has written a memoir (I kind of Knew Edward Gorey), a novel (Well Remembered Movies), a writer's manual (503 Bad Writing Suggestions), a play (Amazing Opportunities Available in Our Town), a zombie book (Tales of the Reanimator's Saloon), a pop culture book (Mama Cass's Golden Caramel Bar), and eight others. Try them. They ain't too bad. And now, with this book, he has dived into art criticism. Hope you enjoyed it.